Nature's Children

SEA LIONS

Mark Shawver

GROLIER
EDUCATIONAL

FACTS IN BRIEF

Classification of North American sea lions

    Class: *Mammalia* (mammals)

    Order: *Pinnipedia* (pinnipeds)

    Family: *Otariidae* (eared seals)

    Genus: *Eumetopias* (Northern Sea Lion);
               Zalophus (California Sea Lion)

    Species: *Eumetopias jubata* (Northern Sea Lion);
               Zalophus californianus (California Sea Lion)

World distribution. Both species are found in the coastal waters on both sides of the Pacific Ocean in the northern hemisphere.

Habitat. Coastal waters; shore.

Distinctive physical characteristics. Strong front flippers for swimming; rear flippers that can be turned forward for walking on land.

Habits. Live in herds; playful in water; migrate seasonally.

Diet. Squid and octopus, fish, shell fish.

Published originally as
"Getting to Know . . . Nature's Children."

This series is approved and recommended by the Federation of Ontario Naturalists.

This library reinforced edition is available exclusively from:

GROLIER
EDUCATIONAL

Sherman Turnpike, Danbury, Connecticut 06816

Contents

If you were to come upon a herd of Sea Lions, you would know it even before you saw them. They are noisy! As they lie about or frolic in the sun or clamber over each other on their way down to the ocean, they are never quiet and seldom still. A colony of Sea Lions is a busy place.

Unfortunately, the only Sea Lions most people see are trained ones in aquarium shows—the ones that balance balls on their noses, blow horns and clap their flippers on command. So let's look and see how these fascinating creatures—so clumsy on land, yet so graceful in the water—live in the wild.

Sea Lions come ashore to mate, breed and bask in the sun.

Puppy Love

Imagine yourself as a baby Sea Lion on a crowded beach where hundreds of Sea Lions have gathered. The world is still very new and you have much to learn. Suddenly, you hear the thunderous growling of two enormous Sea Lions fighting each other. You look up and see that one of them has been given a huge shove and is rolling your way. You are certain to be crushed! But at the last second, you are grabbed by the neck and yanked away to safety. Although you were unaware of it, your mother has been watching over you and has come to your rescue.

Scenes like this happen quite often. For the first five or six months of a Sea Lion's life, its mother is nearby, ready to protect it. Mother and baby spend much of their time lying on the beach, snuggling close together. The little one, called a pup, especially enjoys stretching out on its mother's back for an afternoon nap.

This Sea Lion pup is looking for its mother.

Fin-Footed

Sea Lions belong to a group of animals called pinnipeds. The word *pinniped* means "fin-footed." They were given this name because their feet are effective swimming fins.

Pinnipeds can be divided into three groups. Sea Lions and their close cousins, the Fur Seals, are called eared seals. All other seals are called earless seals. Both kinds of seals are related to the third kind of pinniped, the walrus.

Sea Lion front flipper

Sea Lion back flipper

Sea Lions "haul out" onto rocky shores to rest.

Seal or Sea Lion?

What is the difference between a Sea Lion and most seals? The easiest way to tell is to compare their ears and the way they walk. If the animal has no visible ear flaps and crawls on the land on its stomach like a big caterpillar, it is a seal. If it has small ears on the side of its head and walks on its four flippers, it is a Sea Lion or a Fur Seal.

There are two kinds of Sea Lions along the coast of North America—the Northern Sea Lion and the more common California Sea Lion.

Sea Lions have tiny ear flaps on both sides of their head.

Where They Live

In North America, Sea Lions can be found on the West Coast from the cold waters of Alaska's Bering Sea to the warm tropical waters off California and Mexico. Northern Sea Lions prefer rocky shores, while California Sea Lions like sand or boulder beaches backed by cliffs.

During the fall and winter, the males travel great distances in search of better fishing areas. The females usually stay fairly close to the breeding grounds, teaching their pups how to take care of themselves.

Northern Sea Lion

California Sea Lion

Super Swimmers

A Sea Lion is certainly at its best in the water. Every movement is graceful as it spins and twirls in an underwater ballet. Several thrusts of its flippers can send the Sea Lion gliding through the water at speeds of about 24 to 32 kilometres (15 to 20 miles) per hour.

The Sea Lion has large paddle-like front flippers that are about as long as a man's arm. These flippers flap up and down much like the wings of a bird.

Sea Lions can't breathe underwater so they must surface for air.

The shorter hind flippers are used to steer the animal in the water. On land the hind flippers bend forward and are used for walking.

Sea Lions are great divers and enjoy diving from rocks or boulders at the water's edge. But they must be very careful not to be thrown against the rocks by the crashing waves.

The Sea Lion's streamlined, torpedo-shaped body helps it to be one of nature's best swimmers. Its body glides almost effortlessly through the water.

For getting around on land, the Sea Lion uses all four flippers.

A Fishy Feast

Sea Lions get all of their food from the ocean. They enjoy meals of herring and other kinds of fish, such as cod, flounder and greenling. They also eat squid and octopus.

Sea Lions mostly feed at night. They must move quickly to catch their slippery meals. They capture the prey and hold it tightly in their powerful jaws. They rarely chew their food. Instead they swallow it whole. If the fish is too big to be swallowed in one gulp, the Sea Lion shakes it vigorously to break it into bite-sized pieces.

Usually Sea Lions hunt by themselves or with a few companions. But when a school of herring swims by, many Sea Lions will join in the hunt. Even Sea Lions enjoying an afternoon nap wake up to take part in the fishy feast.

Sometimes a Sea Lion will chase a fish just for the fun of it. It will catch it, let it go, chase it around some more and then let it go again. Sea Lions seem to enjoy this game!

Heavy Weights

Do you know that some Sea Lions may grow to be the size of a small car? In fact, the Northern Sea Lion may weigh up to 900 kilograms (2000 pounds) and reach a length of about three metres (9 feet). The average California Sea Lion, however, is much smaller. It weighs about 250 kilograms (550 pounds) and measures about two and a half metres (8 feet) long. The females are only about one-third the weight of the males.

The male, or bull, Sea Lions are usually brown in color. The females, or cows, are a lighter shade of brown. But when their fur gets wet, Sea Lions look almost black.

Northern Sea Lions may start life tiny, but some grow to be larger than a Polar Bear.

Cozy Warm

The Sea Lion has several ways of staying cozy warm even in chilly waters. A thick layer of fat, called blubber, lies under the Sea Lion's skin. This blubber layer keeps the Sea Lion's body heat in and the cold out.

The Sea Lion has another way of keeping warm, too. It grows a thick coat of fur. The hairs grow so close together that water never gets right down to the skin. Millions of tiny air bubbles trapped in the thick fur also help keep the cold out and the heat in.

In summer, Sea Lions can get too warm. To cool off, they may jump into the water. Sometimes they pant like dogs or wave their flippers in the air like fans. The flippers do not have blubber, so heat from the Sea Lion's body can escape through them.

A fur coat is not a luxury for a Sea Lion. In these icy waters it is a necessity!

New Coats for Old

After a whole year of climbing on rocks, lying on rugged beaches and fighting and playing, a Sea Lion's fur coat becomes very ragged looking. This ragged fur no longer keeps the Sea Lion as warm as it once did. So, each spring when the Sea Lions are on the beaches, their old fur falls out and new fur grows in. Because they are not in the water much at this time of year, missing some of their fur for a few weeks does not seem to bother them. When this process, called molting, is finished the Sea Lion sports a brand-new, shiny coat of fur.

Loafing in the sun.

Underwater Eyes

If you were to dive deep into the ocean, you probably would have trouble seeing. This is because it is dark and murky, and human eyes are not suited to seeing in these conditions. A Sea Lion has large brown eyes with pupils that open up wide to let in more light. This helps it see in the shadowy depths where humans cannot.

As well, Sea Lions have a clear, protective layer that covers their open eyes to protect them when underwater. This layer is what gives a Sea Lion's eyes their soft, gentle look. They also have eyelids much like our own that protect their eyes while on land. And, like us they close their eyes when they sleep.

On land, the Sea Lion's eyes are also protected by tears that help carry away sand or dirt. The tears flow freely down their cheeks, making it seem that Sea Lions are always crying.

Few animals are as graceful in the water as a Sea Lion.

"Seeing" in the Dark

If someone turned out the light, how would you find your way around? You would probably use your hands to feel your way. The night-feeding Sea Lion is often in the dark when it hunts for fish underwater. But, instead of using hands, it feels its way around with the help of its whiskers.

The whiskers are controlled by tiny muscles and are used much like we use our fingers to explore our surroundings. They are equipped with sensitive nerves. Using them, a Sea Lion can tell a slippery octopus from a piece of wood. A trained Sea Lion can even use its whiskers to help balance a ball on the tip of its nose.

The Sea Lion's sensitive whiskers are an important part of its fishing gear.

Other Senses

The Sea Lion is able to close its nostrils so that it does not get a noseful of water when it dives. It does have a keen sense of smell, however. In fact, a mother can tell her pup from all others just by sniffing it.

Sea Lions can hear sounds underwater just as well as they do on land. They have short tube-like ears about the size of your little toe, and they cock their outer ear flaps much the way a dog does to focus in-coming sounds.

A Sea Lion's sense of smell is only useful on land. While underwater its nostrils are closed.

Sea Dogs . . .

Sea Lions are very noisy animals, especially when they are gathered together on a beach. They make an UHH, UHH sound, growl and sometimes even bark. In fact, old-time sailors used to call them sea dogs.

The bark can mean several things. A bull will bark loudly to let other males know to stay away from his territory. The barking sound can also help a mother find a missing pup. She is able to tell her own infant's barking bleat from all the others, even though hundreds of pups may be barking at the same time.

Barking is also used as a warning signal. When danger is near, the bull starts to bark rapidly and run toward the sea. He will soon be followed by other Sea Lions. Sea Lions also bark underwater. This barking can be heard for long distances.

*When a Sea Lion has something to say
it believes in saying it—loud and clear.*

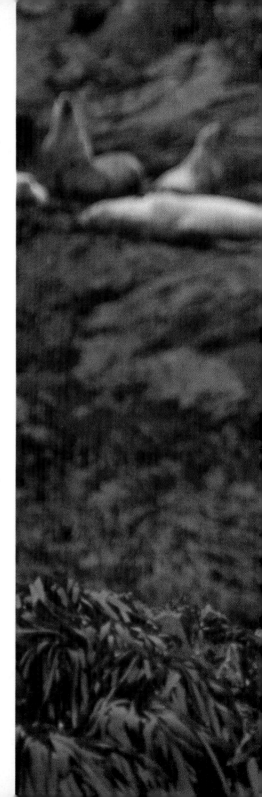

And Sea Lions

You may have wondered why we
call these huge un-lion-like animals
Sea Lions. All you have to do is
hear a Northern Sea Lion roar and
you will instantly know why. If
you closed your eyes you might
think you were in the jungle
hearing a lion roar.

Big Bullies

In the spring, with the coming of warmer weather and longer days, Sea Lions begin to gather on beaches to give birth and to mate. The place where they gather is called a rookery.

Among California Sea Lions, the bulls arrive at the rookery first to claim an area of beach for themselves. This is their territory, and it is where their pups will be born. The females arrive later and settle in a bull's territory. In good territories, there may be 15 or more females. Among Northern Sea Lions, the females arrive first, followed by the bulls.

The group of females in one bull's territory is called a harem. The bull defends his territory by chasing off intruders. Very rarely do the bulls fight, but there is always a lot of barking and growling going on!

The males and females that are too young or too old to mate usually stay on the outskirts of the rookery. If they try to venture in, they will be chased away by one "big bully" after another.

Opposite page:

Northern Sea Lion colony.

Life on the Beach

Sea Lions mate in the summer while on the beaches and the female gives birth to a single pup the following year.

The newborn does not have a cozy nursery as some animals do. Instead, it is born right on the beach among hundreds of other Sea Lions.

The little one looks much like its mother, except that it is smaller and darker. The pup is about 85 to 100 centimetres (33-39 inches) long and weighs about 16 kilograms (35 pounds). Its eyes are wide open and it has a nice shiny coat of fur.

Within a few hours of its birth, the pup begins to drink its mother's milk. Because this milk is so rich, the pup grows very quickly. Although it will nurse for almost a year, it will start eating fish at about six months.

The bull spends most of its time patrolling its territory and pays very little attention to the newborn pups.

Opposite page:

Young Sea Lions cannot yet roar or even bark. Instead they bleat like young lambs.

On the Lookout

Sea Lions have little to fear as they swim, hunt and play in the ocean. However, there are two enemies that the Sea Lion is always on the lookout for. Can you guess who they are?

It is no surprise that one is the shark and the other is the Killer Whale. In a fight with either of these two animals, even the largest of Sea Lions is almost defenseless. Its only chance is to swim quickly or turn quickly to avoid the attacker.

If the Sea Lion can hide in a bed of underwater seaweed or make it to the beach, it may be safe. However, it must still be alert since Killer Whales sometimes slide a little way onto the shore to try to grab an unsuspecting Sea Lion.

Usually, the Sea Lion's enemies take the sick or weak animals which are unable to swim fast enough to get away. Mother Sea Lions must be very watchful to protect their pups.

Mom and her pup should be safe here. The water is too shallow for a shark or a Killer Whale.

Swimming Lessons

How old were you when you took your first swimming lesson? Older than a Sea Lion for sure: a Sea Lion starts swimming when it is only about ten days old. The pup follows its mother to a tidepool, where the water is shallow and calm. They play together, close to the shore. If the pup gets tired, it will often climb up onto its mother's back for a rest.

The pup soon becomes skillful in twisting and turning in the water. This is very important because the next lesson is how to catch a fish! The pup has to learn when to breathe so it will not take water into its lungs. When the mother has had enough playtime, she often carries the pup out of the water in her mouth.

After several weeks in the tidepool and shallows, the pup is ready for the deeper water, farther from shore. It quickly learns to dive below the crashing waves, closing its nose to keep the water out.

Opposite page:

Sea Lion pups stay close to mother's side for the first two weeks of their lives.

Challenges of the Deep

Young Sea Lions are very playful. They toss pebbles back and forth and chase each other around in the water with many leaps and dives. They even play hide and seek in the underwater forest of kelp and seaweed.

Since the layer of blubber that keeps it warm is very thin, the pup can spend only short periods of time in the water. As the pup gets older, the blubber layer grows thicker, allowing it to stay warm on longer swims.

By four months of age, most young Sea Lions are expert swimmers and can stay underwater for about seven minutes. By six months, the pup is ready to swim and hunt for fish on its own, although it stays close to its mother until the following spring. Then it will take its place on the outskirts of the rookery until it is ready to start a family of its own. In the wild, Sea Lions can live to be up to 17 years old and have many pups.

Words to Know

Blubber   A thick layer of fat just below the skin.

Bull   A male Sea Lion.

Cow   A female Sea Lion.

Harem   A group of females in a bull's territory.

Kelp   A type of underwater plant, like seaweed.

Mate   To come together to produce young.

Molting   When an animal loses its fur and it is replaced with new fur.

Nurse   To drink milk from the mother's body.

Pinnipeds   A group of animals whose legs are specially shaped as flippers. Seals, Sea Lions and walruses are pinnipeds.

Pupil   The part of the eye that gets larger or smaller depending on the amount of light.

Rookery   An area on shore where Sea Lions go to mate, give birth and raise their young.

Territory   An area on the beach that a bull claims to be his own.

Tidepool   A small pool of water on the beach.

INDEX

Cover Photo: Herman Giethoorn (Valan Photos)

Photo Credits: Barry Ranford, pages 4, 13, 33; Peter Thomas (Image Finders Photo Agency), pages 6, 23; Herman Giethoorn (Valan Photos), pages 9, 29, 43; Network Stock Photo File, page 10; Tim Fitzharris (First Light Associated Photographers), pages 14, 25, 34; Bruno Kern, pages 17, 26; Don Herrigan (Master File), pages 18; Hälle Flygare (Valan Photos), pages 20-21; J.D. Taylor (Miller Services), pages 30, 44; Wayne Lynch (Master File), pages 36-37, 41; John Foster (Master File), page 38.

Printed and Bound in Italy by Lego SpA